T

BATTLE WITHIN

CHARMAINE

SCOTT

Printed in the United States of America

DEDICATION

I dedicate this book to my children
Jac'Quita, Lewellyn,
and Dalasha.

ACKNOWLEDGMENTS

This book wasn't written to make anyone look bad; I wrote this book in hopes that it would help someone else that is battling with self-love. I struggled with knowing self-love myself all because I was too busy trying to please others as in my family in any way possible. I was looking for approval, wondering way I was always the black sheep. My family always had something negative to say when it came to my offspring and I, telling me to get over what ever happened to me. Well this book will help you get to know why I am me. I still love my family, I just love myself more now. Thanks you Francietta Smith for constantly being in my ear telling me what I didn't want to hear and teaching me how to be a friend. That is probably why you're my only friend. LOL. Thank you Lewellyn for being my number one supporter, I also would like to acknowledge Saudia Mills for everything that you have done for me in the quest of reaching my dream. Love you. Everyone that played a part in my life good or bad. Without you I would not have been able to write this book. I really want to acknowledge my mother because no one is perfect and I pray that our mother daughter bond can grow. I love you mom through everything we go through. Last by not least, Alan from TimeWord Publishing for your contribution. Thank you

Contents

CHAPTER ONE

Christmas Chaos

I guess you could say that I was destined for a tumultuous life from the beginning. I grew up as an only child in my household, but it really should not have been that way because I actually have a biological sister. After my mother discovered that she had a rare blood disease, keeping my sister was no longer an easy task. She chose to let my Aunt Lola, who for some reason was unable to have children, raise my sister as her own. The agreement, from my understanding, was that Aunt Lola was to let my sister know that we were siblings. To her credit, she kept her end of the bargain. We knew that we were siblings and although we didn't grow up in the same household, we still managed to be around one another as much as possible. She would stay over at times and she knew that my mother was also *her biological* mother.

Yet for the most part, I still felt like an only child. There were memories created but most of them only stood out individually. I recall when I was around five years old during the holiday season I, like almost every kid on the planet, was beyond excited without a worry in the world. It was Christmas Eve and the joyful scent of the holidays filled the air. My mother was in the kitchen cooking while listening to Christmas music. Since she appeared distracted, I sneaked around the house trying to find my Christmas gifts. Before long, *jackpot*! I spotted what my mother had gotten me, and I could feel my heart race with excitement in my tiny chest. My plan was to pretend that I was sleep then get up early to open my gifts. That plan failed because instead of faking it, I *actually* fell into a deep sleep. When I awoke, I rushed to where I knew the gifts would be but was stopped dead in my tracks. I discovered that my gifts were not under the tree.

I ran to my mother's room, woke her up, and lead her downstairs to show her that there were no gifts. She became visibly upset calling around, trying to locate her husband. She stomped off to go to a place that I was forbidden to ever go near. In later years, I realized that it was a local crack house. However, she didn't find him there. Not only did he take my gifts, but he also took some food out of the freezer. My mother continued to search but was unable to locate him. What began as the most exciting day ever took a sudden dark turn. Neither of us were able to go back to sleep; we stayed up the rest of the morning in silent disbelief. Hours passed then we got dressed to go down the street to my grandmother's house for dinner. My mother didn't want me to mention anything about her husband stealing my Christmas gifts and the food so, I kept it to myself. When I think about it, I guess that's when I first learned to keep dark secrets tucked away and buried deep inside. 'Right'

Once we arrived, my Aunt Bobbi was the first person I saw. I couldn't hold back. I told her everything that happened. I guess I needed to get it out and say it out loud to make it real. My Aunt talked to my mother about it so perhaps she needed to get it out as well.

That Christmas was a memorable one, but not in a good way. All I received was the ugliest homemade cabbage patch doll that you could ever imagine. I mean this doll was uglier than the infamous Chucky doll. When my mother and I returned home from Christmas dinner, I left the doll at my grandmother's house. That was not by accident.

It was torture for me to watch my other cousins open up their gifts and show me what they received on what should have been the most exciting time of the year for a child. The gifts were visual agony for me and I rebelliously tried to break every last one of them. Everyone talked about how sad it was that I didn't get to open any Christmas gifts because of my mother's husband. The words were empty since nobody volunteered to help my mother replace them. I can't say that I didn't fully understand. Perhaps it was because my mother constantly got caught up with the crack head shenanigans. She would always allow him to come back once he apologized for whatever was done at that time.

A few days later my mother's husband returned home. I could hear them arguing about him stealing our shit. This was pretty normal until I heard the loud noises. I went to see what was going on with them and that's when I saw him strike my mother. I tried to help but certainly, I wasn't any match for a grown ass man.

After they fought, he left again, but that was a routine at my house. They would argue and fight then act like everything was okay. He pretty much came and went as he pleased, and ironically enough, he did the same thing with the penal system. The only difference was that with the penal system, he wasn't able to leave when he felt like it. Every time he went to prison my mother would be right there going to visit and to send him pictures of her.

Looking back, I think she felt as if that was all she had. I never understood why my family wasn't there for my mother like a family should be during those times. I later found out she wasn't the only one in an abusive relationship. As I got older, more and more became clear and although nothing made sense, I could at least understand the insanity of it all. The one relative that wasn't in an abusive relationship thought she was too good for us, and was self-absorbed in my opinion.

Since we all need to feel as if we belong somewhere, I believe my mother, being the black sheep of the family, was looking for acceptance from her mother and her siblings. By not receiving it, her husband was able to come in and mistreat her. I can totally relate to my mother in terms of her feeling like the outcast of the family. I noticed that my mother's siblings treated her as if she was white trash and an embarrassment to their family. Everyone had good jobs and was doing well while my mother lived in the projects and was on government assistance. Perhaps the isolation that I felt was more deep seeded than I realized and was passed down from a woman who was dealing with the same emotions long before I even came into the picture.

CHAPTER TWO

Being Molested

I was about ten years old during the height of the eighties when music television was everything to every single preteen and teenager on the planet. Whenever we had control of the television, we always had MTV on and were glued to the videos. My Aunt Lola was at work, and my sister and I, along with the entire free world, was anxiously awaiting for the premiere of the latest Michael Jackson video, Thriller. You have to realize that this was when MTV ruled but Michael Jackson was still king. The music videos had a way of taking me away from my surroundings to a joyous place where nothing else mattered.

Little did I know, this moment was about to become stained by the reality of my life. The anticipated moment of musical escape took a hard nose dive when my Aunt's husband walked in high and drunk. He was an addict and a full blown one at that. I have no idea what his drug of choice was on that day but he was on something. Crack? Heroin? Alcohol? God only knows. Maybe it was all of it. He was just like my mother's husband in that aspect and that's nothing to be proud of when it comes to decent people. He came into the bedroom that we were in and I was not comfortable with his presence. He sat down on the bed then he started playing around with me.

"Lay down," he said to me. "Let's see if you have any peach fuzz down there."

I had no idea what peach fuzz was. All I knew is that none of it felt right. I looked at my sister but she seemed as confused as I was at that time. She watched him as he pulled my panties to the side then rubbed his fingers up and down my clit.

"You ain't ready yet," he grunted. He then got up and walked out of the bedroom. When he left, he managed to not only take the life out of the room, but another level of innocence that I could never get back. Another commercial came on to announce the countdown of Michael Jackson's World Premiere. But instead of us jumping around and giggling with excitement, we remained still and silent. All the enthusiasm that I had while waiting on the Thriller video vanished into thin air and was replaced with another emotion…fear.

A few days later, my mother came to me and asked if my Aunt Lola's husband had done anything to me. I was frightened at first, and was not going to say anything until she assured me that she already knew. My sister told my

Aunt Lola what happened. Relieved that I would not have to be the first one to talk about what happened, I felt safe and empowered. To just get it out and over with, I told her every detail.

I'm not sure what I expected to happen after that, but I was sure that something would change. However, that was not the case. Nothing was done to him. I still had to see him at my grandmother's house for Sunday dinners and holidays as if nothing happened pretending we were one big happy extended family. Every one that knew acted as if he hadn't done anything wrong.

I later found out that this behavior ran deep in our family. In their minds, they had a valid reason to overlook the incident. My grandmother told my mother to let it go.

"Don't mess up Lola's marriage with that bullshit," were her exact words. At least that's what I was told. I never understood why the matriarch of the family would say that until I got older. I discovered that my grandmother's sister was molested by her Uncle which resulted in a child who was mentally challenged. The birth defect came about because they were close kin. From what I was told, they swept this incident under the family's secret rug and went on with life as if this shit was normal. There was a lot of stuff under that rug and I'm not sure how it all fit.

In my mother's defense, I'm sure she wanted to do something about what happened to me but her hands were tied. My mother listened to her mother without question. After that first encounter with my Aunt's husband, I remember being sent to my Aunt's house to get something for my grandmother that she needed to finish cooking. She lived right through the path so it only took a couple minutes to get to her house from my grandmother's. When I arrived at my Aunt Lola's, no one was there. I opened the door, went in to get what I came for and on my way out, her husband walked in. He locked the door behind him then walked me to the bathroom. He made me perform oral sex on him. I was terrified. I ran back to my grandmother's, put the bag on the table then went to the bathroom.

I rinsed my mouth out over and over. When I felt like I could no longer rinse, I went into one of the bedrooms at my grandmother's and went to sleep. I never mentioned what had happened to me. I didn't tell anyone what happened because I felt as if nothing would be done. No one did anything the first time he touched me so what was going to be different this time. He made sure to point that out to me.

I performed oral sex on him several more times, until he just stopped bothering me. I was told in my adulthood that he was having sex with his blood niece as well. I hate she had to go through that, but she saved me and didn't even know it.

It seemed like when my Aunt's husband stopped, my mother's husband picked up. I was built like a grown woman trapped in a child's body. One day, I was in my room relaxing. My bedroom door opened and my mother's husband walked towards me taking his belt off.

"Get out of my room," I yelled.

My mom was in her bedroom, so I knew she heard me. A few seconds after I screamed at him, we heard my mother come toward my room, so he started hitting me with his belt. My mother asked what was going on and he told her that he caught me playing with my breast. My mother said nothing and just went back into her room. He hit me a couple more times then smiled. Right after he left my room. I jumped up, closed my door and just cried myself to sleep. When I talk to my mother about it, to this current day, she claims she doesn't remember. I can't say if that's the truth or not. Who knows, maybe she doesn't remember, doesn't want to remember or has managed to block it out. One thing is for certain, I sure remember and I always will.

What's even worse is that it wasn't only the males molesting me. I had a female cousin that was slightly older than me, that behaved just as bad as the men in our family. I was at home in my room lying down one evening just relaxing enjoying the peace and quiet. My mother must have left with my cousin's mom so we were alone. She came into my room then got into the bed with me. It wasn't long before she started to rub and hump on me. I immediately pushed her away, but she continued to fondle me. After she reached her climax, she left my room. Not only was I confused but I was hurt that she would do that to me. I never expected that from her. I mean this was my cousin; she was the same one that I use to go to the skating rink on holidays with and it was always fun. Skating was the thing to do and the best part about the rinks were that they turned them into dance clubs after skating was over.

My cousin was right there with me again after the incident in the bedroom. I ignored her for the most part but she didn't get the hint. She came over to me to tell me something but I didn't hear a word she said. The molestation scene was all my mind could focus on that evening. Before I realized it, I swung at her. We got put out of the skating rink for fighting, right before they closed. Our ride was outside waiting on us so we got into the car and didn't mention the fight.

After that, you would think that life would've given me a break but that was not the case. In fact it got worse. One day everyone was at my grandmother's for Sunday dinner. I was about ten or eleven years old at that time. My cousin and I were sent to my mother's apartment to get something for my grandmother. When we got there, I discovered that my mother's husband was there.

"Why you didn't wash the dishes," he said. I ignored him without a response. To my cousin, he said, "You can go back. She'll be there after she finish washing these dishes."

I should point out that there were only two dishes in the sink. "No!" I said. He reached for his belt to whip me. I grabbed a large butcher knife out of the sink. Without the slightest hesitation, I began stabbing him with the knife over and over in a complete rage. That's when he picked up a broom and started hitting me with it in baseball fashion. That did little to stall my aggressive attack. I continued stabbing him with all the strength that I had. My cousin ran down to our grandmother's house to get help. My Aunt and grandmother came and I had no idea how they were going to react. I was shocked to see my grandmother standing there with a brick in her hand.

"If you swing that broom one more time," she warned him. "I will kill you!"

My mother came running into the house. She called the paramedics when she saw all the blood. They assumed it was my blood until they noticed her husband clutching his chest.

After the ambulance arrived, we went to the emergency room. His room was right next to mine so my mother was running from one to the other checking on us. I was not understanding or even trying to understand why on God's earth she felt that it was necessary to check on him. I was thinking, *I'm your child! This should be the last straw. This man beat your daughter with a broom!* Ok, perhaps he got the worst end of this fight, but that was beside the point. Still how in the world could she give a damn about his well-being? The doctor told me that if I would have stabbed him just a little more to the right, he would have been dead. My mother was thanking God but I was thinking about practicing on my hand motions and veering more to the right.

We left the hospital and went home like one big happy dysfunctional family. The silent lesson that I was being taught truly scared me. My mother unknowingly taught me to let a man walk over me as well as my child without any consequences.

I couldn't believe it. Once we got home, I just went to my room and closed the door behind me dismayed and distraught. A few months later my mother's husband jumped on her again. One day David and I, (you'll learn more about

David in the next chapter), went to my house to get my jacket before going to the movies. That's when I noticed that my mother wouldn't look me in my eyes. Mom had her hand up covering her face and it was clear that she wanted to shield me from seeing her. I moved her hand and saw that her eye was swollen and dark.

"Where is your husband?" I asked.

He had just gone out of the back door so I followed him with David right behind me. I went through the narrow path behind the apartment and spotted him.

"Why did you hit my mother?" I asked. Before he could respond, my hand had already transformed into a fist. I swung at him and connected several times. He swung back punching me hard in my chin. That hit left a scar that I am still carrying to this day. That's when David came in swinging in my defense. Once I saw that David was beating his ass, I noticed a vacuum cleaner sitting on the curb on the street that someone was throwing away. I picked it up and began striking my mother's husband on the back several times. My mother's husband was outmatched that day.

We went back to my mother's place and I told her what happened. Instead of thanking us for what we did, she asked me if he was OK. I couldn't believe it. She was sitting on her bed with a swollen black eye still worried if this guy was ok. David looked at me in disbelief. Of course, eventually my mother allowed her husband to return home with her. I think she thought that having a piece of man was better than not having a man at all.

He then left to do what junkies do. When he returned back to the house, I was outside in a storage room that most apartments had at the time. We used it to store items that we didn't need on a daily basis.

I was in the storage room looking for a gun. I knew it was in there so I was determined to find it. My mother's husband entered and closed the door behind him. As soon as he closed the door I put the gun up to his head and pulled the trigger. Divine intervention played a part in our lives that day because the gun jammed. He stared at me but this time there was fear in his eyes. He exited the storage room quicker than when he entered for sure.

After he left, I went to my room to hide the gun. I wasn't worried about him telling my mother that I had a gun because then he'd have to explain why his grown ass was in the storage room with me with the door closed. Needless to say, my issues with him went away and he stayed away from me.

Years later, my mother separated from her deadbeat husband. And one day out of the blue while we were at home, the phone rang. The person on the other line had called to let my mother know that her husband was found dead. Someone had shot him. When my mother hung up, she was distraught but I truly couldn't understand why she was so hurt. She left in tears to go identify the body.

On the day of the funeral, we lined up at his father's house for his final departure. Everyone was visibly upset that this man was dead, but I was not affected in the very least. When we arrived at the church, the ushers seated us in the front. I watched my mother cry over a man who was one of the worst human beings on this earth. I sat with not one tear to give this man. My mind was in another place as I sat there wishing that the preacher would hurry up and finish his dearly departed sermon. I was ready to go home. I felt out of place while his family and my mother were mourning him. In all honesty, I was smiling on the inside and happy that he was now maggot food.

CHAPTER THREE

Teenage Pregnancy

I use to be the classic tomboy. If the guys did it you can rest assure that I did it too or wanted to do it. I played football and shot marbles with the guys in the neighborhood every chance I could get. I was gender blind and boys were simply competition, nothing more.

It was this one guy that would come and just watch us play. One day he came over and introduced himself as John. We began to talk and he made me feel like he cared about what I was going through and would validate me when no one else would. He made me feel safe, and I began to care a little more about my appearance when I came out to play. In my mind, I was in love with him even though I was only twelve and he was eighteen finishing his last year of high school, and I was fresh out the sixth grade. As I look back on our friendship, I realized he was actually a pedophile. He was the same monster as my Aunt's husband and my stepfather. He just came at me with a different approach.

He and his friend Burt would come over every day. In which case, my neighbor Bree started talking to Burt. One evening about six months later, my mother was gone out with her brother's girlfriend which left the house free of adults. I let John come over to visit me. It started off innocent then John started making sexual advances. At first I resisted, but I eventually gave in and allowed the inevitable to happen. A couple months after we had sex, I began to have morning sickness. My mother took me to my pediatrician. The doctor didn't waste any time cutting to the most likely cause of the issue.

As casually as asking what I ate for breakfast, the doctor asked, "Have you been having sexual intercourse?" I just looked at him in silence.

"Mommy, can I talk to the doctor alone," I said.

She left the room and I told the doctor the truth. I took a pregnancy test that very day. While we waited for the results, my mother came back into the room. I nervously waited for the doctor to come and reveal the test results. When he entered the room, it felt as if my heart dropped to the pit of my stomach. He read the results to my mother in the form of an announcement.

"Congratulations, you're gonna be a grandmother," he said.

I couldn't breathe. My mother was pissed but all I could do was laugh and the more I laughed the angrier my mother got. I guess it was just a nervous laugh. Till this current day, when I get nervous, I can't stop smiling.

August 22, 1989, at the age of thirteen, I had my daughter. Unfortunately, John denied that my daughter was his child because by law he could have gone to jail for statutory rape. We did a paternity test because not only was he denying my child but his mother was talking crazy along with her son. Needless to say, the paternity results came back 99.999 percent. Ready or not I had a baby daughter on the way.

After showing John's mother the paternity results, she would drop her off something for Christmas or my daughter's birthday for a couple years then she just stopped. My daughter always wanted a relationship with her father and his side of the family and I didn't want to deny her of that opportunity. Whenever she asked to go over to his house, I would take her.

One day we went to his mother's house but instead of saying hello, as soon as she saw my daughter, the first thing out of her mouth was about how black she was. I couldn't understand how she could be so color struck when her husband was as black as midnight. I was livid; I held my composure and just left. I never bothered those people again.

A couple years later, I met David, my son's father. We both attended, what they called, an alternative school. I was sent to the alternative school because I was always fighting. My attitude was so messed up that it was ridiculous. My defense mechanism was up constantly. You couldn't say anything to me without a confrontation.

David seemed like an angel sent from above. He had a calming effect on me. He was genuine and we would always be somewhere talking when we were supposed to be in school learning. I felt as if he understood me better than anyone. We ended up getting into a relationship and we were together almost twenty-four hours a day.

Like most parents, my mother enjoyed hanging out with her home girl or going out with her boyfriend in the search for happiness. Not saying she was a bad parent but she wasn't focused on being a good parent. Half the time, I had the apartment to myself which made it easy to spend more time with David.

On May 27, 1991, I found out I was pregnant… again! My mother was upset, of course, but my grandmother took the cake. She said that I was nothing but a whore and that my mother needed to take me to get an abortion. My mother listened to her and asked my Uncle J for the abortion money. In the end, Uncle J and David agreed to go half when it was time for me to go to the abortion clinic. But when David was sent to juvenile detention for assault, my mother rescheduled the appointment. When we finally went to the abortion clinic, I was too far along; it was too late for them to perform the procedure. After hearing the news, my mother was upset. But what could she do? She decided to get over her disappointment and helped me raise my children. I knew my mother loved me and I also knew she was embarrassed that I was only 15 with my second child on the way.

The worst part was the dark mark that this left on the family, I guess. Since my family was all about appearances and what other people thought, my young pregnancy was just too embarrassing for them. Maybe she felt that she failed me as a mother and all this could have been avoided if she'd done a better job raising me. Unfortunately, Parenting doesn't come with an instruction manual. She, just like any other mother, did the best she could do with what she had. I wish things could have been better of course, but I don't know anybody who had a perfect childhood. I never expected to be a teenage mother but it is what it is. I finally felt that I had two people that were going to love me unconditionally. When I got pregnant with my second child, my Aunt Carlene told her daughter that she wasn't allowed to be around me.

If she only knew about her own daughter, she would've realized that I wasn't the one she needed to worry about. I wasn't upset that my cousin wasn't allowed around me because at least that assured me that I didn't have to worry about her trying to have sex with me again. But I was upset that she really thought that I was the bad influence and her daughter couldn't do anything wrong. All the time, her daughter was doing shit that was far worst then me being a teenage mother. I hated how I was being treated by my family. They made me feel like I had the plague. At this point, I was used to it and being accustomed to being treated like shit, by your family, is about as pathetic and sad as it gets.

David was released from juvenile detention a month before our son arrived into this world. On January 27, 1992, our son was born and David decided to name him Lewellyn.

My mother and David were at the hospital when my son was born. They were both joking about his size. He really was a big baby. Once I was discharged from the hospital, David was always at my house visiting his son.

We made plans to move in together once I turned eighteen because I was having issues with raising my daughter. At the tender age of fifteen, who wouldn't have issues? My mother played a major role in raising my daughter that at times she went a little overboard. She made me feel like my daughter Kita was hers and I was just her big sister. I fought with my mother constantly about my daughter and it had gotten worse before ever got better.

On my eighteenth birthday, I put in an application for my own apartment in the projects. Because of that, my mother's income from the government was going to stop because I was no longer a minor and considered an adult. I made an agreement with my mother that I would sign over temporary custody of my daughter Kita so that she could continue getting an income. The understanding was that this would be for appearance purposes only and that my daughter would still actually live with me.

My mother agreed with the arrangement and everything seemed to be going perfectly. However, once we signed the custody papers, she flipped the script on me.

"You can't take the baby with you," she said. "I'm gonna keep her with me at my apartment."

I was floored! I felt hurt and betrayed and what began as shock transformed into anger. I began cursing and crying as I made every attempt to take my daughter with me. The scene got worse and my mother took it to the next level. She called the police and after that I had to leave. I cried for days.

When I finally spoke to my mother a week later, she gave me her explanation.

"Listen to me Charmaine," she said, "I'm not risking a chance of going to jail just to let your daughter go with you." If child protective services come by, I need to have her with me."

"That's not good enough for me." I snapped back. "I tried to help you out by giving you temporary custody of my daughter and this is how you do me? I did that for you, so you wouldn't be homeless and you turned on me!"

As angry as I was, I was pretty sure that I would see my daughter again. I knew how things were going to turn out. After all, I grew up with this woman so I knew she hadn't changed. I was positive that she would eventually want to go out and do her thing. Once that happened, she would drop Kita off with me. That's exactly what happened.

There was still a continuous struggle between my mother and me with my daughter. I still had to go through her for everything and it was getting real old real fast. I had to get her permission if I wanted to sign my daughter up for anything or just take her to the doctor. It seemed as soon as I would get used to Kita being at home with me, my mom would come get her especially when she knew child protection services was coming to visit. She would forever give me a hard time for trying to take her back with me.

David and I decided to move to Columbus, Ohio a few years later. But before we left, I went to my mother's apartment to get my daughter. When we arrived at my mother house, I ask her if she had packed up Kita's clothes. Once again even though we were in agreement that I would take my children with David and me to Columbus, she changed her mind. Because I made the mistake of signing temporary custody over to her, there wasn't anything that I could do. I cried uncontrollably while I argued with my mother telling her how I felt that she only wanted my daughter to collect a welfare check and to secure her a place to live in the projects. She never came at me for my son only because his father was involved in his life. She threatened to call the police as I was trying to pull my daughter away from her. My mother had a grip of death on my daughter so I was unable to take her from my mother's cold grip.

After a lot of talking, David finally was able to get me in the car. We left headed for our new life in Columbus. I cried the whole two hour drive there, and after we arrived in Columbus, I was depressed. David had to force me to get up and handle my business because our son still needed me.

"We'll work on getting Kita back." He said.

I knew it would be hard considering my mother's crack head ass husband's sister worked for child protective services. My mother had somebody on the inside to help her paint me as an unfit parent. Eventually as months passed, I convinced her to allow my daughter to come live with me. By then, my mother had done so much damage to my daughter emotionally by telling her I didn't love her and that I loved my son more. I tried my best to show my daughter that what my mother was saying wasn't true, but I think my daughter resented me for taking her brother and leaving her with her grandmother. I tried to explain to her until I was blue in the face that, "Your grandmother tricked me into signing what I thought were temporary custody papers." But she just couldn't understand. I told her, "I only learned shortly after I signed the paperwork that she went to family court for full custody without my knowledge."

Talk about underhanded. I have no one to thank but my mother for the strained relationship between my oldest daughter and me. According to my mother, all my daughter wanted was a mother daughter relationship. Well, she ruined that with all that damn backstabbing so she missed me with that fake ass Dr. Phil bullshit.

Now I had more than just my mother's damage to deal with. At the age of twenty-three, David and I was going through hell. I found out he cheated on me with one of his co-workers but it didn't really hurts as much as it made me angry. And that caused us to grow apart so we separated but were still able to remain friends until he began to slack in his fatherly duties. Now that I was a single mother, money was tight. I had a job working in the healthcare field as a nursing aid assistant but I wasn't generating enough money.

I wasn't a stranger to hustling. It was a female that befriended me who lived in the apartment building next to me. Her kid's father was the "go to man" in Columbus. After speaking with him, I started selling crack. I became one of his regular sellers. When it was time for me to re-up, we agreed to meet over his mother house. When I arrived, he wasn't home but he left the drugs I came for with his brother, Eric.

I thought Eric was cute and funny so I decided to give him my phone number. I had no idea what I was about to get into. I had no clue that this guy was the make-up of Ike Turner, Goldie, Eddie Cain, and Radio (the mentally challenged person played by Cuba Gooding Jr.), rolled into one person. In hindsight, this was one of those situations where I wished I would have left it at hello.

We talked on the phone for a couple months before he came over to my house. We eventually got into a relationship, or so I thought. One night we went out to the bar, Eric had gotten sloppy drunk and picked a fight with me. He slapped diamonds out my ass! I pulled in the parking lot at the store that was located across the street from the bar and put him and his home boy out of my car. He slammed the car door then proceeded to walk back to the bar. As soon as he stepped foot into the parking lot of the bar, I pressed the gas pedal to the floor then released my foot off the break, he looked back seen me headed towards him full speed. He took off running. The bad thing for him was that he wasn't smart enough to zig zag, he ran straight so I easily hit him with my car. He flew six feet in the air. When he came down, he fractured both his legs. I circled around him a few times while he was lying on the concrete. His friend was running on the side of the car screaming while I was circling around Eric.

"Bitch, you ran my nigga over! Bitch, you hit my nigga!"

He yelled as he pretended to try to get into my vehicle. I was confused as to why he couldn't. I mean, the window was down and the car doors were unlocked. I eventually pulled off, went home and went to bed like nothing happened.

A few weeks later, I went over to his sister's house to pick up something. I walked into the house yelling, "Hello!" No one answered. I walked into the kitchen and there Eric stood. He stood by the table with his crutches. My heart dropped; I thought he was going to be on some revenge type shit as he came toward me. I wanted to run but I was either too scared or too curious as to what was about to happen.

He apologized for putting his hands on me then reached out for a hug, I was reluctant at first but I hugged him. We made up and he moved in. No matter how much I didn't want to be like my mother, when I allowed him to move in, I was repeating the same cycle of abuse.

After I got tired of putting up with his disrespectful ways, I moved back to my hometown. Eric and I were on and off for a while. I moved back and forth from Warren to Columbus a few times before I settled back in Warren for several years. Eventually, I ended up getting into a relationship with Daryl an old schoolmate.

CHAPTER FOUR

Baby Girl

Daryl and I were in a relationship for four years when we decided to adopt my cousin's child. My cousin Jasmine was in her late forty's and addicted to crack. She came to Daryl and me with a request. She wanted us to adopt her unborn child because she knew that Daryl was unable to have children but wanted them.

After we decided to go through with the adoption, Daryl hired a lawyer to get the paper work started. October 28, 2006, my phone rang around 4 A.M. I wasn't going to answer it until Daryl mentioned that it could be an emergency.

I finally answered the call. Low and behold, it was my cousin Jasmine calling to tell me that she was in labor. I automatically assumed she was lying, but I still asked her where she was at now. She replied, "Cash spot."

Cash spot is a known trap house where crack addicts go to purchase their product and hang around to smoke it. When I told her that Daryl would pick her up, she told me to hold on that she'll call me back if she needed a ride. This is the perfect example of why I thought she was lying. So I just hung up the phone.

"Who was that?" Daryl asked.

"It was Jasmine," I said. And then told him what she said.

He got excited and told me we needed to pick her up. He couldn't understand why I was so calm and why I refused to pick her up. A few minutes later, my phone rang again, it was her.

She said, "I'm on my way over."

About ten minutes after that call, I heard a car pull up then a door slam. I went to the door and it was Jasmine walking into the house calmly telling me that her water broke. I didn't believe her because she was too damn calm to be in labor. She told me that she had to use the restroom, she went to the bathroom.

"You better not shit my baby out in the toilet!" Daryl yelled out. I thought she went in there to smoke crack. I called my mother and asked her to come over because Jasmine was claiming to be in labor. Once my mother arrived, it seemed like Jasmine's contractions were coming more frequently. Jasmine got on all fours in my living room then asked my mother to pull down her black wind breaker pants. My fiancé couldn't believe that Jasmine was in labor talking that calm, as if she felt no pain. I immediately called 911 once I saw she was actually in labor. While on the phone with the 911 operator, Jasmine gently rolled over on her back then opened her legs.

Daryl and I were nervous as hell while my mother was walking around cussing Jasmine out because she was higher than a giraffe's ass. She was still trying to smoke her crack while giving birth in my living room. The 911 operator asked me if I could see the baby's head. I looked and saw the crown of her head. She advised me to tell Jasmine to push but make sure I was ready to catch the baby. Talk about chaos! My cousin was telling me to hurry up but she's the one in labor, my fiancé was pacing around the house not knowing if he was coming or going, and my mother was still cussing Jasmine out telling her how she needed to get her life together. Meanwhile, I'm shaking like a dice game waiting to catch the baby.

Jasmine pushed a few times and out came the baby! I was so nervous and shaking so bad that I didn't even catch her when she came out. The baby fell straight on the blush rug that we had in our living room. I was yelling for my fiancé to get a string to tie the umbilical cord not realizing that he was already standing next to me with his shoestring. I used the shoestring to tie the umbilical cord. The paramedics finally arrived to take them to the hospital. My cousin Jasmine insisted that they only take the baby because she had, and I quote, "Shit to do." The actual meaning of that was, she wanted to finish smoking her recently purchased crack. The paramedics finally convinced her that they had to take her to the hospital to remove the afterbirth. We arrived at the hospital with Jasmine and the baby.

My mother and Jasmine were still going at it. The baby, whom my fiancé and I named Dalasha, was covered in dry mucus and she never cried. She had to be placed in an incubator for jaundice. Jasmine, my mother, my fiancé and I was in Jasmine's room the entire time. Jasmine kept asking my fiancé to hand her the bag with her clothes in it. After he gave her the bag, she quickly went into the bathroom and yes, you guessed it! She was in the bathroom smoking crack. While she was smoking her stem, (a stem is something that a crack heads uses to smoke their crack out of.), she cracked the door to talk to us. My fiancé couldn't believe that she was in the hospital smoking crack. He looked at me and shook his head in disbelief, left the room to check on our daughter and gave the nurse the paper work for the adoption.

My mother and Jasmine were still going at it when the nurse walked into the room. Tension and crack was in the air so the nurse knew something was going on but she couldn't put her finger on it. She sniffed the air and looked in every direction clearly knowing that the room didn't smell right. She continued to go on with the business at hand and let us know that she needed blood work from Jasmine and that Dalasha still hadn't cried and wouldn't eat.

Jasmine told me that I needed to go check on the baby and to let her know what was going on when I got back from the nursery. I knew she cared about Dalasha but she was just high and didn't care at that time. The blood work came back and at first the nurse said that they didn't find anything in Dalasha's system. When she said that, I felt like Jasmine had dodged a very large bullet. When the nurse returned to the room to let us know that she had made a mistake, she caught Jasmine smoking crack.

Jasmine was escorted out the hospital. The nurse then gave my fiancé and me her room. Our focus was now completely on the baby after the distraction of Jasmine was out of the way. A week almost went by without Dalasha crying. The doctor came in to explain to us that she would not be getting released to leave until they did more tests and made sure that she didn't have any trouble eating; she was on a regular feeding schedule. She would open her eyes and look around but wouldn't make a sound. His mother came up to the hospital to welcome her granddaughter into the world and was overly excited that Daryl finally had a daughter. She purchased almost everything that Dalasha needed. I promise, his mother was the sweetest woman I knew. His cousin also came to visit; he couldn't get over how much Dalasha looked like Daryl even though he wasn't her biological father. Almost two weeks into the hospital stay, they finally discharged us. We arrived at home and Daryl would not put Dalasha down. I had to make him lay her in her bassinette. Daryl took his daughter almost everywhere with him; I didn't have to do too much, if anything. He feed her, bathed her, and put her to bed. He also wouldn't let anyone hold her and if you were lucky enough to do so, you were on a timer.

A few months go by and I started hearing rumors about how Dalasha was being neglected. My cousin's friend called me to let me know exactly who was spreading these lies. You guessed it! It was my cousin Jasmine, Dalasha's biological mother. I told Daryl right away. I couldn't understand why she would do this to us, until Daryl explained that she was doing it out of guilt. When she wasn't smoking crack, she probably couldn't take the pain of giving up her child and not being able to control how she would be raised. Jasmine had three other children as well that she didn't raise due to her addiction. Her mother was stuck raising her other children and was use to Jasmine coming in and out of her children's lives. Jasmine got away with this because her mother allowed that type of behavior but Daryl wasn't having that. He decided that Dalasha was not to be around her biological mother at all. I was wondering how that was going to work considering we're all family and I promised that I would raise Dalasha and Jasmine other daughter, Tia, as sisters. It didn't help the situation when Jasmine's brother called and warned me to stay away from her. He said, she was starting rumors about me and asked him to tell people that Daryl and I were smoking crack together and that I sold everything out of my house for drugs to get high. Yes, it was a complete mess.

I approached Jasmine about the bullshit she was going around town telling people; of course, we ended up getting into a heated argument. After that, I stayed away from her and her immediate family for a while. Daryl said he wasn't shocked about this, he'd heard the horror stories of family members adopting inside the family. You would think I would've known first hand by my sister being adopted by my Aunt and some of the drama that we went through but I guess I was trying to think positive.

Dalasha's first birthday was coming up so I decided to take her over to my grandmother's house on my father's side in order for her to meet her great-grandchild and to let my grandmother know that I was engaged. When I entered the house, I gave her a hug and sat on the couch then took off my daughter's coat.

"So how's life treating you?" my grandmother asked.

"Well…I guess Grammy, (that's what I called my grandmother), the latest it that Daryl and I are getting married."

She had a bewildered look on her face. "Are you two planning on having children of your own?"

"No," I said. "Daryl can't have children."

"Good." she smiled. "Then go ahead and get married."

Now I was confused. *Why would she say that?* So I asked her, "Why would you say that?

"Did you speak with Daryl's mother about the wedding?" she asked.

"Yes," I said.

"What did Mrs. Joyce say?"

"Nothing, but congratulations."

My grandmother decided to break it down to me. That was when I got the unexpected news of a lifetime. I found out that Daryl and I were blood cousins. Not distant cousins! We were close cousins, like first or second cousins. My heart dropped, tears began to form in my eyes.

"Well Charmie," (Charmie was the nickname that only my grandmother used), she said, "as long as you guys don't plan on having children, ya'll will be ok. Cousins get married all the time."

I was really confused then because my grandmother was a very religious person and for her to say that, threw me for a loop. Now I'm wondering if Daryl was adopted because I know my grandmother wouldn't tell me to marry my cousin. We concluded our conversation, and I gave her a hug then left. Before I could pull out her driveway, I called Daryl crying and told him to meet me at home. He was nervous because I'm on the other end of the phone crying uncontrollably. I pulled up in my driveway and before I could get out my car Daryl had pulled up and jumped out of his truck. He walked up on the driver's side and opened the car door. I told him to just grab our daughter and I would tell him what the issue was once we went into the house.

When we entered the house, Daryl put our daughter in her playpen then came into the bathroom where I was sitting on the edge of the tub crying. I told him everything my grandmother said then told him that he needed to talk to his mother. I just knew that he was adopted, because in my heart, I knew my grandmother wouldn't tell me to marry my cousin. I wasn't thinking of the possibility that she just wanted to see me happy.

Daryl called his mother immediately; she confirmed that we were cousins. The news hit us both hard. Now, we were both crying. I couldn't understand for the life of me why no one told us. I mean, we live in a small ass town. My father's people knew, but I was never around them so I had no clue that Daryl and I were family. I never attended one family function that they had. I guess people rather have something to gossip about then having morals. Now my family is turned upside down. I was confused and not knowing if we should do the right thing and call it quits or just follow our hearts. Our relationship took a turn for the worst and I think it was because neither one of us knew how to handle this devastating news. We started fighting constantly. I can remember him coming home one night from the club, Dalasha and I were in the bed sleep. My son had just returned from Columbus with his father. Daryl entered the bedroom punching me, and I was awakened to this horror not knowing what was going on around me. I screamed then the punches stopped. When I opened my eyes, I saw that my son had him by the neck in the air with one hand. I got out the bed and took a few cheap shots punching him in his face; I could smell the liquor coming from his body.

I asked my son to put him down. Once he put Daryl down, Daryl said only five words.

"Why can't I be happy?" He mumbled.

I knew right then that the news of us being cousins was taking a toll on him as much as it was on me. I think my son couldn't understand why I didn't just throw him out. I didn't let him know about us being cousins. Daryl continued to talk crazy until he passed out, but my son slept in my room on the floor until he felt like it was safe for him to leave. The next day when I got up for work, Daryl was sitting at the edge of the bed in a daze.

A few weeks later, Daryl came home once again drunk with two of his homeboys. He came in the house talking shit about him spending money on this and that for me. I sat on the couch counting my own money without responding. As soon as I was done counting, Daryl snatched my money out of my hand while my Uncle was standing there. After he did that, I noticed my Uncle was about to step in but I shook my head no. Daryl turned to walk away, and I took the picture that was hanging on the wall and slammed it against his head. After that, I grabbed a can of frozen Bud Ice and cracked it against his skull. He stumbled forward before falling down in between the couch and end table. I got on top of him and just started swinging. He start yelling out loud begging my Uncle to get me off of him. My Uncle tried to grab me laughing. Saying, “I can’t get her!”

My Uncle finally convinced me to get up off of him. Once I got up, I asked Daryl to give me my money back. He refused. So while Daryl and my Uncle talked and walked towards the door to go outside, I calmly walked to our bedroom and grabbed his forty-five. I went outside and my Uncle spotted me with the gun, he just stepped to the side. Daryl was about to get into his truck when he saw me standing by the side door with the gun. He froze. Daryl’s homeboy also stood frozen by the passenger door. I started shooting and the next thing I know, his homeboy took off running. I emptied the clip. I didn’t shoot him but I did shoot up his truck.

After that, my sister said Daryl called her fiancé to ask for a gun because he just got shot at by someone. Her fiancé asked him by who and Daryl told him that it was me. My sister’s fiancé started laughing and refused to give Daryl a gun. He told him that I was probably just trying to scare him. He also told him that he knew if I wanted to shot him, I would have. That’s when my sister chimed in telling her fiancé that, I was not playing that Daryl just better thank God that my aim was terrible.

A few days later, Daryl returned home apologizing and gave me my money back. Daryl didn't need the money because he sold drugs too. As crazy as it may sound, I think we were both trying to make the other person leave. Neither one of us wanted to end the relationship but couldn't deal with being family. Didn't Gladys Knight say that first?

Anyway, I remember waking up, giving him a high five and saying, "What's up cuz! We still doing this incest shit?"

The look on his face went dead as if he had just lost his best friend. One day, he just decided that he knew the answer.

"Fuck it!" he said. "We just gon get married. I'm from West Virginia anyway, that's what we do!"

I wasn't feeling it though. I couldn't shake the fact that he was my cousin; this shit was mental torture. A few months before his mother passed away, I had to call her over to the house at 4 A.M. Daryl had just purchased a Mossberg pump a few days prior and was ready to use it. He was crying talking about killing himself while I was trying to calm him down and the scene just went from dark to darker. He said that he was going to kill me first then himself, because he knew I was going to leave him. That's when I called his mother just to let her hear her son over the phone. I didn't want to say anything so I wouldn't agitate him.

Finally, I heard the sound of her car pulling up! It was the most joyous noise I'd ever heard. I had never felt so relieved! She brought hope into what was a hopeless situation moments before. I just knew Daryl would put the gun down once his mother came inside. He went on for about an hour before finally giving his mother the gun.

About a month after that, Daryl's mother went into the hospital and passed away shortly after Christmas. Daryl took it hard and felt like he was being punished by God. Daryl and I stayed together till March of the following year then we finally split up. Even though we knew it was for the best, I became his nemesis. We still tried to co-parent Dalasha but how can you co-parent knowing that you're cousins? Three months later, while drunk, he and his friend got into an argument inside of a bar. They both pulled out their guns and shot each other multiple times. Daryl was rushed to Cleveland Clinic hospital in critical condition. I was conflicted on what to do, but the love I had for him took over and I once again totally dismissed the fact that we were cousins. I consistently went to the hospital to visit him. I would talk to him, washed his face and put on his favorite preacher, Rev. Creflo Dollar, the televangelist from Georgia.

About a month later, Daryl started to come around. I would go up to the hospital faithfully. He wouldn't let the nurses do anything for him; he would tell them that his wife was coming.

"She'll bath me and walk me to the bathroom," he said.

At that point, I knew we needed to talk because we both got pulled back into listening to our hearts. We discussed the fact that we couldn't be together but he would still be in Dalasha's life. I felt like the conversation went rather well. Apparently, I was fooled because instead of him asking for help to go to the restroom, he pulled a fast one. He let it blow out of spite. Since I know that he knew that he was unable to hold his bowels, honestly, I felt he purposely had a bowel movement on himself just so I would have to stay and clean it up instead of me leaving him at the hospital. Regardless though, I continued to visit him until he was discharged. Then it was back to the war of the roses, and trust me, the scent was not sweet.

I went into a deep depression. It was during that period that for the first time in my life, I tried cocaine. I guess it's not a surprise. They say people who have been molested end up using some kind of drug to numb the pain. Fortunately, this only went on for three weeks. Three strong weeks! At this point, I was what they called a powder head, I guess. In the end, that shit wasn't for me. I fell into a statistic for a short period of time but had to pull away from it.

Here's one of the reasons why. I went out one night partying, snorting powder, popping pills, and drinking Absolute Vodka and woke up the next morning butt ass naked in bed with Daryl unable to remember how we got there. I got out of bed went to the bathroom and looked in the mirror. I just shook my head repeating to myself that this wasn't me. I went back to my bedroom, threw the eight ball of coke away that was on my dresser, woke Daryl up and kicked him out of my house.

After that, I decided to move back to Columbus with Dalasha. Soon, I was back in a relationship with Eric. I'm sure you remember him. Eric was now in his forties, and had the mental maturity of a sixteen year old but I didn't care. Even though I knew it wasn't the best decision for me, I was in a bad place emotionally and didn't want to be alone after finding out my fiancé was my cousin and having to go through all the extra drama it caused.

Eric was someone I was familiar with and I knew for sure that we weren't related. So for a while, Eric made me forget about what went on with Daryl and me. As time passed, reality kicked in and I began to see my current relationship with Eric with a much clearer vision. He was a straight bum. Granted, a bum with a job but a bum nonetheless. But it's crazy! Even though I knew Eric was no good, I had convinced myself that I loved him instead of letting it be what it was…a rebound. During this time, I learned so many other horrible things about Eric. One thing in particular was that he was jealous of me. Right?! Why would a nigga be jealous of a female? Let me tell you why. Because he was an alcoholic, an undercover powder head, a womanizer, and a male whore who was still chasing his dream of being a famous rapper. He couldn't stand the fact I was coming up and always on my hustle. Always grinding. He was a complete waste of time. I guess I stayed with him hoping he would grow up. Though dysfunctional, he was at least somewhat of a father for Dalasha. Speaking of Dalasha, this was around the time she started to miss Daryl and the time she found out she was adopted.

At a young age, Dalasha was very talented and intelligent. She was eight going on fifty. She loved to entertain. Knowing that, I decided to submit her in to a

Disney audition. Well, a week before we were to leave for Orlando for her audition, I decided to let her go to Warren with my sister for the weekend. When she returned home, I met my sister at the gas station to pick her up. Dalasha got into my truck crying like she'd lost her best friend. I asked her why she was crying. She told me that Jasmine and other immediate family members told her that Jasmine was her biological mother. In my opinion, they didn't do this out of love for my daughter. If it were from a place of love, they would have respected me as her mother and spoke with me first. That was a straight, "fuck you," to me. I prayed that this wouldn't mess with her grades since she was a straight a student. I was furious and all I could see was red. I was so upset with them because they took it upon themselves to tell her something that was solely up to my discretion and that was my responsibility when the time was appropriate. They had the nerve to think that it was okay like they did nothing wrong. She was only eight years old. Why anyone would do that to an eight year old child is beyond me.

That moment took me all the way back and reminded me of my childhood growing up. I was always made to feel like I was less than. It was so bad that I felt even my sister's kids and my cousin's kids were raised to shit on Charmaine as well as my own offspring. Excuse me as I go off on a bit of a tangent… As far back as I can remember, when they asses needed something, they never had a problem asking me. My dumb ass would be Johnny on the spot. Because I wanted to feel accepted and loved, I always made a point to be there for them. As time went on, I grew sick and tired of my family playing games with my life and now Dalasha's life.

I have to give credit where credit is due though. When my daughter was going through this stage, Eric was right there for her. He wasn't a great father figure either but now he was all she had. At her age, it was only natural for her to start calling him dad. And… I didn't stop her. I knew it may not have been the best decision to allow her to call him dad. But looking at her, I could see that feeling like she actually had a father put a smile on her face. So, I went along with that temporary fix. Through all of this, I began to recognize that I was passing, to another generation, the same curse my mother passed down to me. Sometimes, the smallest things can shed the greatest light on a situation. Mine was an article about self-esteem. This is when I realized that my own self-esteem wasn't even a blip on the charts. The article said that a person only dates at the level of their self-esteem. Those words hit me hard. If that was the truth, then I was screwed.

I realized my daughter had watched me go from one abusive relationship to another. She saw me leave Daryl for Eric, who was not only a terrible partner, but he was also a self-absorbed sex addict. Sometimes I wondered if he was on the down low. He seemed to constantly desire to have anal sex, in which I found to be pretty weird yet it brought out my inner Scorpio.

Regardless of our poor relationship, his mother and I were pretty cool. Well, that is, until the day Eric used my truck and afterwards I found an earring in it that didn't belong to me. I couldn't believe it. I was so upset and had no one to talk to because everyone that truly loved me was sick and tired of hearing me complain about Eric. So I called his mother to talk to her about it. Even though I knew that was her son, I thought as an older woman, she would offer some well needed words of advice. To say the least, I found her response to be that of unconcern, which was totally unexpected. I was at a loss of words. But here it is in all its glory (and I quote), "Charmaine, you know he does music, he raps and has a lot of female friends. If it were me, I wouldn't even bring it up to him, but maybe that's just because I'm grown."

She wouldn't bring it up just because she's grown? Who thinks like that? I couldn't believe what I'd just heard.

That's when my eyes opened even wider, and I knew that she just wanted any woman to take her son off of her hands. Before I knew it and without thinking, I said, "Maybe, people need to do a better job raising their sons." After that, I felt she didn't care for me anymore. Eric and I continued to mess around a little while longer. Once again proving the article to be true. But moving right along, the straw that finally broke the camel's back was when he cheated on me with a girl who ultimately lied about being pregnant with his twins. I knew she really wasn't pregnant but that ain't none of my business. But if you're interested, just keep reading. She continued with the lie for the length of a full term pregnancy. She even purchased clothes for the "twins." She kept up with everything knowing that she wasn't actually pregnant. His sister and I tried to tell his dumb ass, but he refused to believe us.

Here's the kicker, according to her, she went into the hospital and the doctor took the twins. She said an hour later, they died. She told him that she didn't call him because she was mourning. She didn't have a birth or a death certificate and never produced one either. I personally went to the vital statistics site and there was no record of the birth of the twins. This situation made me look at myself even harder, wondering what was so fucked up in me that I would continue to allow myself to be mixed up in a so called relationship with someone that doesn't even have common sense. The problem was clear and I had to face the fact that apparently, I didn't love myself. For whatever reason, I needed to be around people who I felt needed me. I had the mother complex big time and wanted to save everybody, but wasn't willing to save myself. I just recently completely removed Eric from my life while taking time to work on myself. What I've learned so far is that the more I love me, the less I want to be bothered with Eric or other men like him.

CHAPTER FIVE

Family

Warren, Ohio was my home when I met MarShawn. He hung out with my cousin and Uncle since they were in the same motorcycle club. MarShawn would try to talk to me but I ignored him until one day we were at the bar talking. I decided to go out to dinner with him the next day. We talked for a couple months before he gave me some inside information.

One day he told me that my cousin and Uncle told him not to talk to me because I was nothing but trouble. They said that I would have him in nothing but unwanted drama. I couldn't believe that my cousin said that. As for my Uncle, I really didn't know him that well so his opinion didn't matter. He was just going off of what he heard. He was fully grown when he came over my grandmother's house one day with his father who was my granddad. In all honesty, I didn't even know my granddad either; I just heard stories on how he told my grandmother that he was going to the store for some bread and never came back.

Still I was hurt when I was told what was said about me. This was especially hurtful since my cousin nor Uncle thought about telling me that MarShawn was a married man.

How fucked up was that? They cared more about someone that was not family to go tell him nothing but negative things about me. That showed me once again that they didn't love me enough to make sure I wouldn't get emotionally hurt by this married man. I didn't know that he was married because we would hang out all the time in public, displaying affection around his nieces and nephews. He told me that he wasn't in a relationship so I had no reason not to believe him.

My mother came over my house one day while MarShawn was lying in the bed chilling. When he wasn't around, she gave me a warning. She told me not to sleep with him. I was wondering why she would say that. It just made no sense to me. Why would that even matter to her?

Since I had been with MarShawn for months, my mother had plenty time to tell me that and to give me her reasons way before now. I asked her why did she bring that up, and all she said was, *"Am I'm too late?"* Um…fuck yes! She knew we were hanging out for months. We're both adults so why wouldn't we have already slept together? I pressed her for an answer but she never said why she told me not to sleep with him. I told MarShawn what she had said and he told me in his own way what my mother was trying to say to me.

"You see," he said, "People think the worst of people without even knowing the situation. People are always name calling and shaming folks calling them a hoe when they didn't even know the entire story, and it happened when her daughter was ten years old so…"

"Wait nigga," I said. "Who is she and what happened? Are you telling me you slept with my mother?"

He never answered.

A few weeks later, I saw his wife at the grocery store where she worked. She was talking to someone else but loud enough for me to hear. "You know how women do," she said. She said, how it's fucked up when a man fucks a mother and her daughter. I continued to shop because like he said, I didn't know the whole story and no one cared to tell me. Months later my cousin, her sister and I went out. I ran into MarShawn while we were outside smoking a cigarette. He walked up to me and told me that he loved me.

"You know that you're tripping by not speaking to me," he said.

He grabbed me by my neck and choked me. When he let go of my neck, he told me to wait right here while he goes to get his gun to kill me. My cousin Sarah was buzzed and began to talk shit to him, telling him that he had life fucked up, if he thought that he was going to do anything to me.

Now my cousin is about 5'4 talking shit to Marshawn who was about 6 feet tall. Sarah's Sister, Kim, stepped in and advised us that we should leave because he looked like he was serious. We left and a few days later I ran into MarShawn again.

I asked him if he was seriously going to kill me and with a straight face he said, "Yes." Needless to say, I stayed clear away from MarShawn. At some point while my daughter was going through her mental disorder, I moved back to Columbus, Ohio. My mother thought that I wasn't doing enough for Kita. She called my cousin Valerie talking bad about me, telling Valerie that I never gave a fuck about my daughter and that she was going to call the police and send them to my house. Valerie was confused and shocked as to why my mother would call her talking about her own child as bad as she did. Valarie called me as soon as she got off the phone with my mother to tell me what was said. My feelings were hurt but once again I was so use to my family shitting on me that I became numb to it.

If they knew of anyone who was close to me and truly loved me, it was as if, they would try to sabotage that relationship. It was like they didn't want me to have anybody in my corner. The way my family treated me is so fucked up that people who loved me started to notice and stopped fucking with my family. My Aunt and my mother along with one of my cousins tried to tell me how bad Valerie and her daughters would talk about me, and even had the nerve to say my best friend tried to get them to take my kids from me twenty years ago. If my best friend was trying to get my family to take my kids from me, why wait twenty years later to tell me?

My cousin lived with my Aunt Carlene while he was trying to get his life together. When my Aunt tried to convince him how fucked up I was, he couldn't understand her reasoning for bashing me. The attempt to make me look bad backfired; it made him want to get to know me even more. We would hang out when he was sober and just talk.

One day out of the blue he said he understood why nobody in the family wanted him to hang around me and why they didn't support my son while he was in college playing football. My son became quite the football player in college.

They would brag about my son but never actually went to a football game. *Never!* They would say they wanted to go to one of his games but for some reason, they never made it. They also never came to any of his high school games so I don't know why I expected them to travel to New York for one of his games. My cousin broke down his conclusion. He said because our family is so into appearances and what other people thought about them, they could never accept you. How can they let people know that the reason you went through so much fucked up shit was because they were a fucked up family. They abandoned you when you needed them most, especially when you were a kid. The more he talked the more watery my eyes got.

"I've always been on my own," I said in a voice barely above a whisper as if it was hard to admit it.

"Not anymore," he said. "You always have me to look at as a big brother now."

My cousin was their when I was told that my father might not be my real father. I was crushed not because I found out that my mother possibly lied to me, but because of what my fiancé and I went through. Hell, because we thought we were cousins, we couldn't be together. All of that could have been avoided had, once again, my mother told me the truth. After finding this information out, my cousin Valerie and her daughters tried to help me piece things together. With the little information I had, I went on the internet trying to find my people. I found a guy in Detroit that was supposed to be the son of the man who I just found out was my father. I inboxed him and he responded rather quickly. My cousin and I drove to Detroit to meet the guy that might be my blood brother. When we arrived at his house, he was thrilled to see me. The first thing he said was I look more like his dad then he does. The sad thing was the man that might be my father died six months before my mother told me about him.

I was so confused, because there was a picture in my grandmother house of someone from my dad's side of the family that looked just like me. I asked my grandmother if that was me in the picture.

"No," she said, "that's your cousin."

My alleged brother showed me a picture of his father and I really resembled him. When I returned from Detroit I tried to speak with my mother about getting a D.N.A test because I wanted to know who I belonged to in terms of my real bloodline. As soon as I started asking her about it, she started crying. I felt bad because my mother was sitting there in tears. She didn't want to take the test and asked me not to say anything about it until she passed away. Once again, I put my emotions to the side for my mother, even though I felt like it was my right to know the truth. I convinced myself that since I never had a father anyway, it didn't matter at this point.

In the end, I can say that I've gone through pure hell! I've experienced life threatening situations, I should've been in prison for murder, and avoided being a statistic. I guess it took me all that time to realize that in order to get through all of this I am proven a fighter and I have the courage to push through. I didn't need my family or those jacked up men in my life. I was *never* alone. Instead of allowing my head to hang down in shame, embarrassment, and low self-esteem… all I had to do was look up and *within.* While all this was going on in the summer of 2012 my Cousin Sarah's daughter passed away from an asthma attack. The night before she passed, she had stayed the night at my house. Just me and her. She had a ball. She was the sweetest little girl, always happy. That next day I receive a phone call that Ky Ky was in Children's hospital. Shc had slipped into a comma because she went to long without oxygen. She remained in a comatose state for a few weeks before her parents decided to take her off of life support. I couldn't stand seeing my cousin Sarah go through this. I tried to be there for her the best why I could. I would try to convince her that everything was going to be okay. I tried to be strong, but the day Ky Ky passed, I was in charge of getting her ready for the funeral home by bathing her. That was one of the hardest things I ever had to do. I thought I had it together emotionally, but I was wrong. After I bathed Ky Ky, we were all leaving, and I was walking to my car, my stomach started to hurt. I had to turn around and go back into the hospital and as soon as I made it into the public restroom, I shitted on myself. I had to throw my damn panties and socks away. It was my nerves! I was shitting and crying. I finally made it home to bathe myself. Soon after, I headed over to Valerie's house, Sarah's mother. Ky Ky was my girl. That's why I don't like getting close to people because either God takes them from you or ya'll just fall apart. Ky Ky's services were beautiful. She received a princess sendoff. She had the horse and buggy and a gown only a princess could wear. Months later, I got a tattoo on my leg in remembrance of Ky Ky. Its roses and butterflies. Those were her favorite things. She was such a girly girl.

CHAPTER SIX

Home Visit

I was in my early twenty's when I went home to visit for Labor Day. Everyone was at my mother house having a great time, listening to music, playing cards. My family actually let my friend on the grill. You couldn't tell him that he couldn't cook.

We were on the porch talking when my Aunt Lola's husband walked up as if he was invited. I didn't say anything because I didn't want to cause a scene. First thing my family would have said is that girl's crazy, she know she didn't have to do that. Everything was still going well until my Aunt Lola's husband picked my niece up and sat her on his lap. I lost it.

My Uncle Daylyn asked me what was wrong but I ignored him. My Aunt Lola's husband kept telling my Uncle that everything was ok. He knew why I was upset. Once the tears started flowing from my eyes, it was over for him. I punched him as hard as I could and the hit resulted in knocking him unconscious. I was still trying to kick his ass but someone grabbed me. When my Aunt's husband awoke, he tried to take off running that's when my favorite cousin

Sarah came up out her shoes and chased him down the street. My mother ran after Sarah. She actually caught her and brought her back to the house. My cousin was still hyped. Her mother tried to calm her down, then she accidently pushed her mother into the wall. Sarah was going off.

"This is fucked up!" She said. "Nobody had Charmaine's back when that freaky muthafucka did what he did."

She was a hundred percent right. He knew what he did was wrong. That's why he wasn't tripping when I went off. My Uncle just sat at the kitchen table claiming he didn't know what happened. I can't say that he was not being honest; I just don't understand how he didn't know when his sister and my grandmother knew what happened. My Aunt Bobbi had the nerve to say something totally out of line.

"Why that girl do that?" she said. "She could have killed that man."

She said that because when I knocked him out, he fell and hit his head on a rock. The rock was in my mother's yard for decoration. I was hurt that she said that because once again what about me? Why couldn't she say, I understand why she did that? I'm just happy my niece didn't kill him. I feel like no one has ever had my back. It feels like my family is always putting the blame on the victim. I guess that's the easiest way for them to deal with it.

No one ever reached out to me to see if I was okay, if I needed help or therapy… nothing. All I ever heard from them growing up is, Charmaine is out of control. Charmaine is crazy. Charmaine needs an ass whooping. Charmaine this. Charmaine that. I was sick and tired of hearing it.

When it was time for me to head back home, my cousin Rob decided he wanted to move to Columbus. I allowed him to come stay with me so my son and I went to my Aunt Carlene's house to pick him up. I walked into the basement and saw my Aunt Bobbi's son, my Uncle Daylyn, my Aunt Carlene, and her daughter. We began talking about what happened and my Aunt told me to just get over it.

My Aunt Bobbi's son even had a few words to say. I really couldn't believe he had the nerve to open his mouth considering that word on the street is that he's also a rapist and allegedly raped a close relative and gotten her pregnant.

There was no surprise that his mother just wouldn't believe that her son would do something like that. Even though he's been a drug addict since he was at least eleven years old from what I was told. His mother did not want to accept the hard truth about her son. My son was so taken back by what my Aunt said to me that he injected himself into the conversation too.

"If getting over bad experiences are so easy," he said to my Aunt, "then why can't you get over your husband's death?"

The room got quiet until my cousin Rob spoke. "Imagine how Charmaine felt? Every time she went through a situation and needed her family, no one was there for her!"

He even broke it down to her about how he felt when we were getting close and my Aunt tried to convince him that I was crazy. My Aunt Carlene's daughter chimed in telling me that I needed to leave their house.

"She always starting some shit," she said while looking at me.

"Shut up," I said. "Before I throw your ass under the bus."

My cousin just looked at me. We decided to leave to make sure things wouldn't get physical.

CHAPTER SEVEN

Dealing with Mental Illness

I lived in Columbus while my oldest daughter remained living in our hometown. I was stretched across my bed when my mother called me with some disturbing news. She told me that my daughter had to be rushed to the hospital. The news became even worse as she gave me more details. My daughter was admitted on to psych ward.

My mother proceeded to tell me about what lead up to her being admitted to the hospital. Apparently, her behavior became odd and erratic. My daughter was roaming from room to room pouring water on the beds. When she entered my mother's room, she poured the water in her face while she was sleeping. My mother said she thought that she was drowning until she opened her eyes and saw my daughter standing over her bed. Before the police arrived, my daughter tried to get butt naked and run outside. In the process of my mother trying to physically stop her, my mother hurt herself. Somehow a big piece of skin came off her hand which made me worry because my mom has an auto immune disease and I didn't know if she would have a hard time healing. The police arrived, but even they had trouble.

They had to call for back up and the officer told my mother that Kita was as strong as an ox.

My mother was pleading with the officers not to shoot her. It took seven male officers and two paramedics to subdue her. My mother also told me that she may have known the cause of her behavior. She thought that my daughter's ex-boyfriend slipped her a mickey. I wish I could say that I was shocked but I wasn't. I never liked him or his mother. His personality was a lot like his body odor. It was out this world. He constantly talked about how he was a hit-man and how he ran shit in Florida, where he was originally from.

There was always something off about that entire family in my opinion. His grandmother had Halloween decorations up all year round. His brother was slipped a mickey and was always off his medication so his behavior was pretty odd most of the time. His sister was gay so she did her own thing. As for his mother, she hung out with her son as if they were friends instead of mother and son.

I jumped up out of bed and flew back home as fast as I could. The instant I saw my daughter, tears flowed from my eyes. I cried so hard I could hardly breathe. My daughter had no idea what was going on with her and was no longer the same.

She was discharged a few days later, and diagnosed with a drug induced schizophrenia bipolar disorder. When she returned to her grandmother's house, she appeared to be okay to me. Kita told me that she was sitting down watching Braxton Family Value and the people in the show just start looking demonic to her. She then said that she saw the floor opening up. To this day she will not watch that show.

I returned home after speaking with my daughter and determined that – aside from some lingering effects from the mickey – I thought she would get better and be okay. My mother would call me with stories of what my daughter did or said. In my mother's opinion, she wasn't getting any better. She kept telling me that she needed to be on some medication. I refused to believe her. After a couple months of listening to my mother's concerns, I finally convinced my daughter to move to Columbus with me. Once she arrived everything seemed fine but after a week into her living with me, I began to notice the things that my mother was talking about. Even then, I still refused to believe that something was wrong with my daughter's mental health.

I was in the shower one day and I heard my daughter Dalasha yelling. "No! Kita no!" I rushed out the shower to see what was going on with them. My daughter Kita was trying to put a lit cigarette in the kitchen cabinet. I asked her why was she doing that but she was acting as if she didn't have a clue about what I was asking her. I got upset and yelled at her. I told her to stop acting stupid! Stop acting like you don't have any common sense! She continued to walk to her bedroom as if I wasn't even talking to her.

In a stark contrast to my oldest born, my son gave me very little, if any problems, growing up. He graduated from college, moved to Columbus, and got an apartment with his high school friend Sam, and his cousin Robert. Lewellyn has always been a good boy and now a good man. He's been able to be the mediator between me and he sister, Kita.

It was on a rainy Sunday morning when I decided to go to the grocery store to pick up a few items for Sunday dinner. I left Kita and Dalasha at the house. As soon as I pulled into the parking lot at the grocery store, my cell phone rang. It was my youngest daughter, Dalasha. She was calling to tell me that her sister was acting strange. While I was talking to her, I heard someone in the back ground barking like a dog.

"Dalasha," I said, "who is that barking?"

"It's Kita mommy, and she is crawling around the house."

"What?" I said.

"Yeah, momma she also tried to tell me that I was a dog and then picked me up and start throwing me on the furniture."

While heading back home, I called my son to tell him to meet me at the house. As soon as I walked in, Kita was acting as if nothing happened. I asked her what was going on but she acted as if I was speaking a foreign language. Soon her brother walked in with his friend Ron. Ron and Kita were best friends growing up. He tried to turn their friendship into a relationship but that ended when we moved back to Warren.

Kita saw Ron walk through the door and quickly went into the bathroom. Her brother followed her asking her what was going on with her. I let them talk for a few minutes without intervening. Her brother would be able to get more information from her. I thought that she would open up to him, but instead she insisted everything her sister said she wasn't true. She said that she was only playing with her sister and wasn't barking like a dog. I had to let her know that I was on the phone and I heard her barking.

Her brother convinced me to call 911 to get her evaluated again. I was hesitant at first because I still felt like there wasn't anything wrong with her. I honestly felt that she was seeking attention. I called for the paramedics but unfortunately, the police arrived first. She began to flip out, crying, yelling that we were trying to get rid of her and that I called the police to kill her because I wanted her out of my life. At this point, everybody was crying trying to calm her down. The police officers convinced her to go to the hospital by threatening to take her to jail, if she continued to refuse treatment. We knew that they couldn't do that but she finally agreed to go to the hospital but she refused to get in the police cruiser. The officers agreed to let her ride in her brother's car while they escorted them there. They walked her in so that she wouldn't have to wait to go in the back to be seen.

After Dalasha got dressed, we went to the hospital to find out what was going on with her. The doctor asked me for some background information on my daughter. They ended up keeping her for observation on the psych floor. When my daughter heard that she was going to be admitted, she got upset and started cussing and fussing saying that she wasn't staying and that they couldn't force her to stay. She told the doctor that they only wanted to keep her so they could rape and kill her. At that point, the doctor put a seventy-two hour hold on her. Even while all this was happening right in front of me, I still refused to believe that something was wrong with my daughter. I wouldn't allow myself to believe that Kita wasn't the same Kita.

Once she was admitted, she called every five minutes asking me to come pick her up. When I told her that I couldn't, she would get upset and tell me how much I didn't love her and I wanted her dead. She did that for a couple days before she finally calmed down. I convinced her to participate in the group sessions that they held every evening for the patients. She began to attend therapy but her biggest complaint was that she wasn't anything like the people in there and nothing was wrong with her. She said, there were people walking around looking like zombies from the medication. Other patients walked around with helmets on to stop them from being able to harm themselves and a few patients had Tourette's syndrome. After going into her eighth day, the doctor released her with some medication and insisted that she follow up with a psychologist.

On the way home, we had a conversation about her mental health.

"I don't think that anything is wrong with you," I said. "I think that you're just seeking attention."

She always felt that I loved my son more because she was with my mother the majority of the time. I constantly would try to let her know that wasn't the case. I explained to her again how her grandmother tricked me into signing over custody and how I fought with my mother over her. For a few days, she was doing well. Yet, in the back of my mind, I knew something was wrong, I didn't want to face it or admit it. I remained in denial.

She would tell me odd things all of the time. Things like, people were watching her, trying to kill her, and how she was seeing witches. It was going into the second year since she had been diagnosed before I began to acknowledge her mental disease. I wanted my Kita back. Still desperate to get the old Kita back, I called my boyfriend's sister, Joann, who practices Wicca and herbal holistic cures. I hoped she could help Kita. I dropped Kita off over Joann's house praying for a miracle. When I returned, Joann suggested that I purchase a few items for Kita's protection.

I told my mother about it. She swore up and down that Joann was evil and how I shouldn't trust her because she was my boyfriend's, Eric, sister. My mother was convinced that she helped him put some kind of spell on me because of the constant bullshit I'd put up with from him.

"Mom," I said. "This is not what you think. Joann isn't some evil witch that just sits around the house putting curses on people. She is all about women's empowerment."

My mother did not look convinced.

"Just because she's a Wiccan and has the same mother as Eric," I continued, "doesn't automatically make her a bad person."

She went on and on so much that she talked my daughter out of trying what Joann suggested. Kita wouldn't take her prescribed medication regularly either for nothing. It was frustrating for me, trying to work, raise my youngest daughter, and constantly dealing with my oldest daughter's delusions. Little did I know, I had not seen the worst of it.

I was in California, when I received a phone call informing me that my daughter stabbed her best friend. I was stunned. I never thought my daughter was capable of physically hurting someone. She had it set in her mind that her friend had slapped me and that I was dying from cancer. I was between a rock and a hard place. Of course, without a doubt, I love my daughter; however, I also want to follow my dreams. While I was getting ready to go to a B.E.T Awards after party with my cousin, I received the call that my daughter had flipped out. I was stressing because she left in my vehicle after she stabbed her friend. I called my daughter's cell phone repeatedly until her friend answered it. My daughter left her cell phone at her friend's house, now I had no way to get in touch with her. I called my friend to help me locate my daughter. The way the police are now, I feared that she would get killed if she got pulled over. My child has mental issues and sometimes depending on the officer, their first reaction may be to shot now and ask questions later. My friend called me back to let me now that she'd located my daughter. I thanked God immediately; if something were to happen to my children, I wouldn't know what to do with myself. I called another cousin of mine to pick up my daughter and take her to my mother's house until I returned from California. I was shocked but thankful when she agreed to do it. I returned back to Ohio, picked my daughter up, then headed to Columbus. On the way back home, my daughter and I talked about her getting help, staying on her medication, and going to therapy. I finally accepted the fact that my daughter really needed professional help. I realized my daughter, as I use to know her, was gone but I didn't understand why God would allow this to happen to her. When this situation first happened, not only did I refuse to believe it but subconsciously, I think I was embarrassed that my daughter wasn't herself anymore.

That warped thinking may have been in my blood. I grew up with a family that cared more about what other people thought than their own family. Being real, I'm sure this was passed down to me. As much as I tried to refuse it, I still had some of their messed up ways. Everything started going well for a while until my daughter once again stop taking her medicine. She would have random outburst of odd behaviors or swear up and down that someone raped her. It got to the point that if it actually happened, I would've a hard time believing her. I would talk to my best friend constantly about my daughter and she always said that I was doing more harm than good to her by keeping her with me instead of having her around people that were on her same mental level. I felt that if I put her in a group home or any kind of mental facility, I would be abandoning her. Considering everything that I went through when she was a child, I didn't want her to feel like I gave up on her again. Even though I knew my friend was right, the guilt from my mother taking her from me wouldn't allow me to leave here again.

My mother kept trying to convince Kita to move back to Warren. Depressed and I assume feeling defeated, she eventually gave in and moved with my mother. My daughter, Dalasha, went to Warren for school break to be with her sister. When she came back home, she told me that my mother was telling my daughter that I didn't love her and that Kita should have just been her daughter because I was never attached to her. I couldn't believe that my mother would stoop so low…again. I thought we were past this. My mother denied saying it, and I didn't know what to believe.

I definitely wouldn't put it past her. My daughter Kita is now on the shot for her condition which last her for a month so she doesn't have to take the pills any longer. She's slowly getting better, I feel that my mother hinders Kita. She wants to work but my mother keeps discouraging it by telling her she will mess up her social security benefits. I totally disagree with her logic or actually lack of logic.

CHAPTER EIGHT

Moving On

After dealing with my ex, Eric, I was forced to look within. Even though I was livid about the way he treated me, I had to face some hard facts. I could only blame myself at the end of the day because I allowed it to happen. I had to drop to my knees and pray for God to take all this anger and hatred from my heart. It was a slow process. After I started caring less about Eric, I was able to realize that I was so focused on hating him more than I was focused on loving myself. I thought about all the things that Eric said and physically done to me. And how afterwards, he would come over like everything was okay, even though, I told him that I was tired of his bullshit and that it was over. Because he knew that I was all talk, everything I said to him fell on deaf ears. I would constantly say that it was over but continued to let him back into my life. It actually wasn't all about him. It had more to with my vision. I had this vision of a family in my head that he was surly unable to give me but it was still there. He would come to my house as if he'd never done anything wrong, asking me to cook. I cooked his ass something to eat alright. At this point, I was in that fuck him stage. Whatever I could do to make his life a living hell, I did it until I realized it was taking too much of my energy to hate him the way I did. Eventually, I put my big girl panties on and went on about my business. Eric is out of my life now. I'm finally learning how to love myself and stop putting others before me. I also had to remove a few family members out of my life for my happiness to continue to outgrow the bitterness.

CHAPTER NINE

Depression

I suffer from depression. I had moments when I felt like I wanted to kill myself, and life wasn't worth living. What got me through were my kids. I couldn't be selfish to them, and I knew if something happened to me no one in my family would treat them right. I fought to get all the dark thoughts out of my mind. I would stay in the bed for days, struggling to get up and had a hard time just making it a productive day. I decided to go get professional help, because I knew I could no longer deal with this alone. Deciding to go to a psychiatrist wasn't an easy decision. My culture just does not believe in getting mental assistance. Black people are supposed to be strong and fix their own problems. I would have severe panic attacks so I really needed help. Therapy was very helpful because I was able to get a lot of things off my chest. I was prescribed Xanax for my anxiety and some other medication for my depression.

The medicine didn't agree with me. It kept me unaware of my surroundings, so because of that reason, I decided to stop taking it and deal with my depression. When I would feel myself getting depressed, I would try to keep myself busy which actually works for me.

CHAPTER TEN

Dreams

I remember when I discovered that I could sing. I would walk around the house pretending like I was performing on soul train or some other music show. One Sunday morning, my mother had a house full. All my cousins had stayed the night. The next morning my mother got up and was cooking breakfast for everyone. We were all in the kitchen trying to help. It was the early 90's. The female group En Vogue, who had a hit song titled Hold On, came on the radio. I began to sing as if I was performing at the B.E.T awards. After I finished singing, I looked at my cousin Boy Boy and noticed that tears were rolling down his cheek. He made me think I sounded terrible until he asked me to sing it again. When I said no, he got upset. That's when I knew I put on one hell of a show. A few weeks later, I was over my grandmother's house with my cousin Pam who was close in age. I told her that I wanted to sing gospel music. She started to laugh and said, "Yeah okay."

That crushed me. I never spoke about it again and just left it a distant memory. I began to write constantly. That was my escape. I use to write whatever came to my mind and developed a passion for it. Once again, I went to a family member and disclosed to her how I felt about writing. I told her, when I became a grown-up, I wanted to make movies. Again I received discouraging words but I would still write then throw it away when I was finished. I didn't want anyone to laugh at what I wrote. Now in my adulthood, I still would write but I wouldn't tell anybody because I felt like my work wasn't good enough so I continued to throw whatever I wrote away. One day I was speaking with my cousin Sadeesha about her dreams. She wanted to be a singer. I encouraged her to follow her dreams and when you make it come get me to be your back up singer. My cousin Rob ask me why settle on being someone backup singer when you can sing too. I thought about what he said and came to the conclusion that maybe I heard I couldn't or I shouldn't do this or that knocked so much, my self-esteem was broken down and made me think that I was never good enough to be anything other than Charmaine. That's the reason why I always told my kids that they were able to do anything they desired! If my children said, mommy, I wanna be Santa Claus when I grow up. I would say, baby be the best damn Santa Claus you can be. I never wanted my children to feel they weren't good enough. Anyway back to my cousin Sadeesha, in 2004, she moved to California to pursue her dreams and goals. One day we were on the phone and she told me that she was going to be on Sundays Best. I was excited for her, as it was going to be on B.E.T. When it was time for the show to come on, I was glued to the television. When she came on to sing, I smiled ear to ear hoping she would make it all the way through. Even though she didn't win, she never gave up. Years later in 2016, I started writing my Petty Girls series in which I posted on Facebook. I wanted to see how people would respond to my writing skills. My cousin really enjoyed reading them. I spoke with her about some other projects that I was working on and she invited me to come out to California to network. By now she'd been in Cali for some years and had met some amazing people that could possibly help me get to the next level. I flew out to California taking her up on her offer and once I arrived I really didn't want to come back to Ohio. We went to a B.E.T after party. I never in a million years would have thought that I would be standing next to Tyrese, Wiz Khalifa or Big Tigger but there I was little ole Charmaine mingling amongst the stars. That encouraged me to chase my dreams harder. Dammit! Nothing anyone can say will kill my spirits in the pursuit of my happiness. It's time for me to live for me. I am a mother of three and a grandmother and I refuse to leave this earth without having a legacy to leave behind for my children. I was always told it's better late than never.

Made in the USA
Lexington, KY
29 November 2019

57828073R00052